CHRISTMAS AND NEW YEAR TRADITIONS

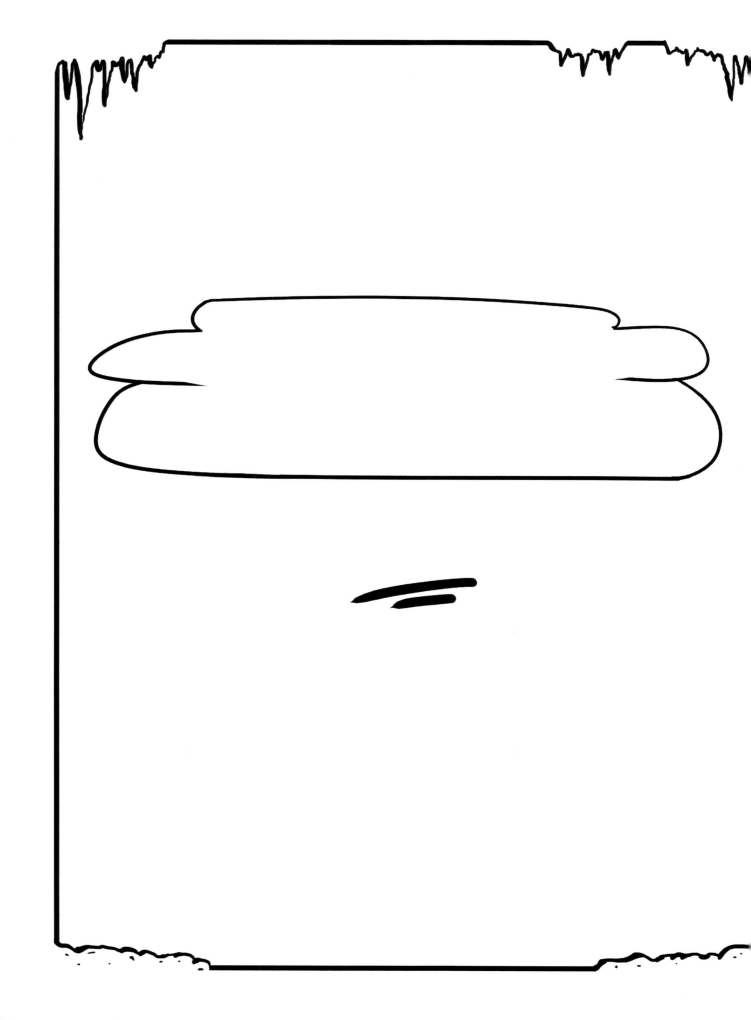

WINTER HOLIDAYS AROUND THE WORLD

A Funny Read Aloud Picture Book About Holiday Gif
and Traditions of the Holiday Season
For Kids And Adults

TABLE OF CONTENTS

CHRISTMAS AND WINTER HOLIDAYS AROUND THE WORLD

A Funny Read Aloud Picture Book About Holiday Gifts and Traditions of the Holiday Season For Kids And Adults

Introduction

On the last day at school and the teacher finally announces the Christmas holidays. As soon as you hear the word «Christmas,» the first thing you probably think of is that your next 12 days are going to be spent surrounded by friends and family. Your run in the corridor with your friends and soon your parents come to pick you up. Just as you know, the festive season has finally arrived.

Many of the traditions associated with Christmas date back to earlier festivals, such as exchanging gifts, indulging in massive amounts of food, and decorating a tree. A season when we may spend quality time with our family while creating holiday decorations and other crafts, singing Christmas carols, listening to lovely Christmas stories, and baking delicious delicacies.

But what is so special about this day? Why is everything themed in red, white, and green? Who is Santa Claus? Why is this day so grand that we get so many holidays from school?

Well, the answer lies in the history of Christmas.

So Christmas is the day of celebration for Christians worldwide who believe that Jesus Christ was born on December 25.

But wait. Who are Christians? And who is Jesus Christ?

History of Christmas:

Christians are the people who believe in Jesus Christ and that he is the son of God and came on Earth in a human form. According to shared Christian beliefs, Christ was born on Christmas, that is, December 25. In short, you can say that it was the day when God's son was born on Earth, according to most of the Christian communities.

If you are a Christian, you already know some of the things priorly mentioned above. And if not, it will be a great reading time both for you and your parents!

The word «Christmas»:

Christmas comes from Middle English Cristemasse, which in turn comes from Old English Cristes-messe, literally meaning Christ's Mass.

Christmas in different cultures around the world:

The word «culture» to the collective or shared behavior and tradition patterns of a particular group of people or society. Think of culture as a circle in which many people live together and follow a daily routine related to their beliefs and traditions.

In this «circle,» many things are included that influence how that particular group lives their life. The most common factors are food, language, clothing, and religion.

Christmas is celebrated all over the world and among billions of people. But not every country needs to celebrate this big day with the same traditions and rituals. Every country that celebrates Christmas celebrates it differently as compared to all other countries.

Christmas and New Year:

December is full of festive anticipation across the globe. Christmas is not the only blissful moment people worldwide are waiting for at the end of the year. New Year celebrations are another reason both children and parents are super excited to spend quality time together, play games watching movies, or do anything related to having a good time with the family. In short, the new year is a cherry on top, along with Christmas celebrations.

The new year is one of the oldest celebrations in the West (in countries like Europe, the United States of America, and Australia).

New Year's Day, especially in the West, is celebrated by various traditions and customs. The night before, known as New Year's Eve, is filled with enthusiastic celebrations and massive dinners.

They stay up late and keep track of how many seconds are left before midnight. It is common for people to organize firework shows, and they will gather outside at midnight to watch the beautiful sky as it strikes 12 and it is suddenly all so brightly lit by the sparks and colors.

Why should you read this book?

As mentioned above, every country celebrates Christmas in its ways, according to its traditions. Each practice that you will read throughout the book will make you learn something you never knew and encourage you to learn more about a country and how the people live there. Moreover, the best thing that you will learn while reading this book is appreciating and respecting various cultures and traditions worldwide. Knowing how each country celebrates Christmas is both informative and exciting.

CHAPTER 1:

The people in Finland believe that Santa Claus lives in «Korvatunturi,» also known as «Lapland.» Korvatunturi is situated in the northern part of Finland, the northern part of the Arctic Circle. Children from all around the world send the most precious letters full of wishes to Santa Claus in Finland.

There is also a «Christmas Land» in the northern area of Finland. They say that Santa Claus lives near that tourist theme park.

The Legend of Joulupukki:

The other possible name for Santa Claus in Finland is **«Joulupukki,» which** translates into «Christmas Goat.»

According to the legend, the Christmas Goat was traditionally a Yule Goat who was frightening and asked for presents from everyone. But as the infinite time passed, the Yule itself started giving presents to children! Joulupukki is raised with a reindeer and leaves the Christmas gifts under the Christmas tree. But naughty kids might end up having a big bag of coal!

It is also believed that Joulpukki has a wife named «Joulumuori,» which translates into «Old Lady Christmas,» but there is significantly less evidence of her.

Be careful in what tone you wish in. Evil spirits can hear you wishing to Joulupukki. However, the old man has outstanding listening skills. Make sure to whisper to him all your wishes!

Fun fact: In Finland, Happy Christmas/Merry Christmas is **'Hyvää joulua.'**

Three important days:

Finnish people purify their houses and apartments ready for the three significant days of Christmas that are:

1. Christmas Eve
2. Christmas Day
3. Boxing Day

Food:

In Finland, Christmas is not only for human beings but also for animals. Farmers hang up a huge pile of wheat on a tree. In this way, birds can enjoy their festive meals too. Besides wheat stems, the people of Finland also hang nuts along with pieces of suet (that is a hard white fat on kidneys of sheep and other cattle animals) in bags from the branches.

Christmas Eve:

It is the most important and remarkable day over Christmas. Rice porridge and plum juice are a specialty for a morning drink. The tree is then bought and adorned (if not already). At lunchtime, the city mayor of Turku broadcasts «the peace of Christmas» on radio and television.

Visiting the ones who are gone:

Another traditional practice on Christmas in Finland is visiting the departed. Most of the people go to the cemeteries and visit the graves of their loved ones. Since some of the cemeteries are huge, police monitor the massive traffic surrounding the graves. Candle lanterns for the departed family members are left in the cemetery. The whole cemetery glows as all the people who visited the graves leave the glowing lanterns. The experience is nearly magical, and the presence of the ancestors is vaguely felt.

Christmas Sauna:

Other people like a sauna on Christmas Eve.

More food:

The majority of the Christmas feast is either served in the late afternoon or early evening. Finland's traditional appetizer for Christmas is Lutefish (salt fish), but it is not common nowadays.

The main Christmas meal is eaten in the early evening. The main meal is a leg of pork served with mashed potato traditionally baked slowly in birch-bark boxes in the oven with similarly cooked mashed swede. Casseroles containing different vegetables, including rutabaga, carrot, and potato, are also typical. Cured salmon is very popular, and some people also have turkey. Dessert is baked rice pudding/porridge eaten with spiced plum jam. One almond is hidden in the pudding. Whoever finds the almond will be lucky for the following year.

After the meal, Joulupukki (Santa) might visit the house! When he comes in with his sack, he asks if any children are living there. They reply very loudly! Next then asks if they have been good all through the year. When they are given their presents, the whole family gathers to watch the fun of opening. After opening some presents, it's time to go to bed - but some people like to stay up all night to see Christmas Day arrive!

The main course of the Christmas dinner is served in the evening hours. The main course consists of a leg of pig served with mashed potato traditionally baked slowly.

Christmas Day is significantly less busy, with most families opting to stay at home and relax. On Boxing Day, many individuals want to go out and celebrate. It is common to go skiing or to skate on the flat landscape,

CHAPTER 2:

SCOTLAND

CLEANING THE HOUSE FROM TOP TO BOTTOM HAS LONG BEEN A NEW YEAR'S EVE RITUAL

GREAT EMPHASIS WAS PLACED ON SWEEPING OUT THE FIREPLACE

THE MOST DESIRED GUEST ON JANUARY 1 IS A BRUNETTE WHO CROSSES THE THRESHOLD NOT EMPTY-HANDED.

GUESTS ATTENDING THE PARTY SHOULD BRING WITH THEM CHARCOAL, WHICH THEY LATER THROW INTO THE FIREPLACE FOR GOOD LUCK

Scotland is breathtakingly beautiful in winters. If you ever get a chance to witness Christmas in Scotland, you will take a deep breath and notice how crisp and pure the air is. The lights of the Christmas markets glitter like gems over the city, enticing pleased shoppers inside to spend the holiday season there. Hotels all around the country are lighting fires and shutting the curtains to create a warm, welcome ambiance for exhausted travelers as the winter weather approaches. While the rest of the country prepares for the year's biggest festival, **Hogmanay,** when Scotland ushers in the new year, Christmas in Scotland provides all you need for a memorable holiday break.

The lights from the crowded stalls glimmer and twinkle like pearls. A Christmas market is unrivaled when it comes to generating a festive atmosphere. There are big European-style markets in Glasgow and Edinburgh, food booths, rides, entertainment, and other activities. The cities of Perth and Aberdeen, and many other places across the country are hosting similar winter events.

Hogmanay and Stonehaven Fireballs:

Scotland's New Year's celebration, known as Hogmanay, is so busy and fun that the entire country is shut down for two days! There will be a celebration in every town and city, and it will typically feature ceilidh dancing, delicious food, and fireworks at the end of the night. The fireworks display on New Year's Eve in Edinburgh is one of the most stunning in the world. Fire festivals are hosted at a few locations in Scotland, including Comrie and Stonehaven.

At the start of the New Year, Stonehaven excites the enthusiasm of the public. In Aberdeenshire, this fireballs event is one of many winter fire festivals that are distinctive to Scotland. It is a spectacular sight to witness.

Traditionally, a purification ceremony was performed to extinguish any evil spirits that remained from the previous year, allowing the New Year to begin clean and purified. People watch all this in astonishment as, just before midnight, a piper leads a procession down the street. At the same time, participants hoist fireballs above their heads in the ultimate test of courage and power. These fireballs represent the sun, and according to the legends, it is also believed that these «suns» are thrown into the sea, so that the ones who live in there get light and warmth.

Yule cake:

To this day, baking a Yule cake is one of the genuinely ancient customs that Scots continue to pass down the generations. Most of the families prepare a loaf of unleavened Yule bread. Everything about Christmas traditions, including this bread, has one distinctive characteristic: the person who discovers a small piece of jewelry or any other small item buried within the bread will be blessed with good fortune for the rest of the year.

Rowan twig:

Scottish people also believe in burning a rowan twig. According to a legend, the reason for doing so is to «burn» any unpleasant feelings that may exist between friends and family members.

The first footer:

Christmas Day's first footer is the individual who is the first person to arrive at their residence on Christmas Day. First footers bring presents such as whisky, salt, coal, and bread to the house to bless all of the guests staying there. Moreover, if the first footer is a brunette, it is believed that they will bring good luck.

Rich ingredients such as raisins, currants, almonds, citrus peel, allspice, ginger, cinnamon, and black pepper are all included in the famous and delicious first footer gift recipe, which is also known as **black buns.**

In many ways, Scottish Christmas traditions are comparable to those seen in other Western countries. People decorate their homes with lights, put a Christmas tree in the window, and a wreath on the door for the holiday season (wassailing). On Christmas Eve, children write letters to Santa Claus and leave him something to eat (such as a mince pie) and drink (such as sherry or whisky) when he comes to visit them late at night.

CHAPTER 3:

Spain comes to life every year between December 24 and January 6, when the country celebrates Christmas, known as *Navidad* in Spanish. This time of year, everyone wants to fill their holidays with delight, excitement, and family harmony. January 6 is a significant event in Spain known as **el Da de los Tres Reyes Magos** (also known as **Epiphany or Three Kings' Day** in the United States).

Spanish Christmas Lottery:

Although Christmas Eve is not until December 24, Christmas in Spain always occurs a few days earlier, on December 22. School kids perform a live broadcast of the drawing and announcement of the winning numbers for the extremely popular **Spanish Christmas Lottery,** which takes place on that day. Many Spaniards purchase lottery tickets in the weeks leading up to this event, and they wait to see if their number is drawn as the lucky one that year.

As soon as the lottery winners are revealed, the holiday season is officially underway, and everyone begins to make finishing arrangements for the vast celebrations ahead.

Nochebuena:

Christmas Eve, also known as **Nochebuena** in Spanish, is celebrated on December 24 and is often family-oriented. On Christmas Eve, members of the extended family usually assemble to have a feast consisting of meat, traditional delicacies that are rarely eaten throughout the year, and several types of desserts.

Nochebuena is a very joyful night in many houses, especially those with children because it is the night when Santa Claus, in Spanish called Papá Noel, gives gifts to all children who have been good throughout the year. Some regions of Spain have their traditions: in the Basque Country, **Olentzero** is the one who leaves the gifts, while children in Catalonia and **Aragón** receive gifts from Tió de Nadal (Tito the Nadal).

Nochevieja:

Nochevieja, as it is known in Spanish, is the celebration of the end of the year and the beginning of a new one. It is celebrated on December 31, which is New Year's Eve. However, the festive season does not come to an end there!

After a long year, we've finally arrived at December 31, the last day of the year. In contrast to Nochebuena (Christmas Eve), which is spent with family, Nochevieja (New Year's Eve) is enjoyed.

The 12 lucky grapes:

Before the clock strikes midnight, the final moments are spent by Spaniards preparing to ring in the new year, following dinner, and chatting with family and friends. People congregate in plazas or in their houses to consume the **12 uvas de la Suerte** (12 lucky grapes). Everyone consumes 12 grapes during the last 12 seconds of the year to ensure that luck will be on their side for the remainder of the year.

Misa del Gallo:

After supper, committed Catholics have an important occasion to attend: **the Misa del Gallo,** a special midnight mass held every year to commemorate the feast of St. Joseph. Churchgoers celebrate the birth of the Son of God by singing well-known and traditional Christmas carols, which are accompanied by guitars, hand drums, and tambourines, among other instruments.

Even after the massive Christmas Eve supper, the family gathers on Christmas Day to eat again, though not nearly as much as they did the night before. Families with young children, in particular, should take advantage of this opportunity to discover what Papá Noel has brought them all. A sea of children fills the streets as they experiment with their new roller skates, bikes, and remote-control cars.

Christmas in Catalonia:

Catalonia, Spain, has a Christmas character known as **'Tió de Nadal'** or the Christmas log, also known as the **'Caga tió' (the pooping log!)**.

It is a small hollow log hoisted up on two legs and painted with a happy smile on one end. From December 8 (the Feast of the Immaculate Conception), Catalan households provide the log with a few morsels of food to 'consume' and a blanket to keep it warm during the winter months. On Christmas Day or Christmas Eve, the log then 'dispenses' little gifts to the children. To aid in the log's 'digestion,' people sing a specific song and hit it with sticks, and as a result, the log drips sweets, nuts, and dried fruits. When a piece of garlic or an onion falls out of the log, it means that all of the delicacies for the year have been consumed. The Caga tió can also be found in many parts of Spain, particularly in the Aragon region, known as the 'Tizón de Nadal.'

Nativity Scenes:

In Catalonia and throughout Spain, **Nativity scenes** (also known as «Pesebres») are pretty famous. In addition, several towns host 'Pastorets,' which are large-scale plays or presentations on the Christmas story, specifically the birth of Jesus. There are a lot of music and Bible readings during the service.

'El Caganer':

'El Caganer,' which also translates as 'the poo-er,' is a peculiar character who is famous and customary in the Catalan town of Peebles. And, yes, it is a representation of a human going to the bathroom!

On the majority of occasions, it depicts a Catalan villager crouching with their trousers/pants down, wearing the customary red Catalan cap (known as a barretina). Year after year, new versions of El Caganer are currently being produced, often featuring the likes of celebrities and politicians! This figure has been a feature of Catalan nativity scenes since the early 18th century when it first appeared.

Tres Reyes Magos:

For the younger members of a Spanish household, January 5 is an overly exciting day. The entire day is dedicated to a spectacular celebration in which gigantic floats parade through the streets, accompanied by bands of musicians and visual artists, as well as people dressed in costumes and, most importantly, the Three Kings, who wave to all the youngsters in their respective cities. Following the procession, families come home for an early dinner, allowing the youngsters to clean their shoes and store them in the living room while they eat. As a result, when the Three Wise Men arrive at the house in the small hours of the morning, they will identify where to leave the gifts for each member of the family.

CHAPTER 4:

Although most Vietnamese are Buddhist, they do not prevent themselves from celebrating the occasion of Christmas. People in Vietnam are enthusiastic about having a good time and look forward to all kinds of festivals as opportunities to get together and celebrate.

For most Vietnamese, Christmas is more of a curiosity than a religious occasion, and it is not recognized as an official holiday in their country. However, because Christians account for 8% of the population, you will discover many spiritual components, such as Midnight Mass on Christmas Eve, throughout the city. You will still see Christmas decorations illuminating the skylines of major cities, as well as carols playing in stores and markets. Here is how to spend Christmas in Vietnam, with everything from delectable feasts to stunning nativity presentations.

But since Christmas isn't the main focus, all of their attention goes to celebrating the New Year.

Tet Ong Cong:

Vietnamese prepare the traditional offerings, particularly the carps (a type of fish), on the 23rd of the last month of the lunar calendar to greet the gods and goddesses who reside at their residence throughout the year. This is an incredibly significant activity for the Vietnamese.

There is a big reason why Vietnamese greet the Kitchen Gods with carps: they believe that buying and freeing the carps in the river would assist the Kitchen Gods in their journey to heaven. These gods then report all of what has happened throughout the year to the one known as «The King of Heaven.» All of this happens on East Day, which often takes place one week before the Tet holidays.

When the gods return to Earth on the last day of the year, these carps are transformed into dragons.

The New Year Tree:

When the lunar calendar year comes to an end, it is customary for Vietnamese people to build a bamboo pole, known as a **«Neu tree,»** in front of their homes to get rid of evil spirits, worship gods, and pray for good fortune in the coming year. They take it down on the 7th day of the New Year to say goodbye to their ancestors in the afterlife.

The New Year tree serves as a guide for the spirits of ancestors who have returned from the other side to celebrate the New Year with humans. The bells serve to frighten away evil spirits from entering the house. The residents also take further precautions, such as drawing a bow on their courtyard walls with lime powder. According to legend, the arrows of the bow are intended to scare away evil spirits.

Food:

During the Lunar New Year celebrations, every Vietnamese household has a dish filled with five different fruits on the ancestor's shrine. The fruits are bright and have symbolic significance, and elevate the celebration of the New Year.

According to Asian mythology, the world comprises five essential elements: metal, wood, water, fire, and Earth. Metal is the most common element, followed by wood, water, fire, and Earth. This concept can be represented in various ways, one of which is the plate of fruits placed on the family altar at the beginning of the year. Additionally, the dish of fruits symbolizes the hope for abundant harvests and prosperity.

A plate of fruits generally contains five to eight different varieties of fruit: a bunch of bananas, a grapefruit, a «Buddha's-hand» fruit, a lemon, oranges, tangerines, apples, or persimmons, to name a few examples of what to expect. Families select only the most attractive fruits, which are then arranged in a pyramid shape.

Decorations:

Like Vietnam Hanoi and Ho Chi Minh City, the major cities go all out for Christmas celebrations. Vietnamese Christmas decorations, including dazzling lights, garlands, candy canes, snowflakes, and other festive accents, can be found in abundance throughout the city's department stores, hotels, and streets. The experience of wandering the streets and marveling at the kaleidoscope of lights and colors is an utterly amazing one.

Also, you'll hear Christmas carols playing in the background of shops, restaurants, and hotels, and you'll be shocked at how many Christmas carols the locals know, even though Christmas isn't officially celebrated here.

If you are in Ho Chi Minh City, make sure to visit Nguyen Hue Walking Street, which boasts the largest and most colorful decorations. The streets will be jammed with ecstatic people, and it will be a genuinely magical environment.

CHAPTER 5:

Fairy Befana with her broom and Santa

Christmas celebrations in Italy start from December 1. This lasts until the day of the Epiphany, which falls on January 6. Children, in particular, look forward to the beginning of the Christmas season in December, when Christmas trees are standing upright and residences are decked out for the occasion.

The nativity crib scene:

When it comes to celebrating Christmas in Italy, the Nativity crib scene is one of the most important aspects to remember. It was St. Francis of Assisi who, in 1223, did the practice of using a Nativity tableau to assist communicate the Christmas story significantly. It is common for many Italian families to have a Nativity scene in their homes.

Naples, Italy, is world-renowned for its Nativity scenes, which can be found around the city. These are referred to as **'Presepe Napoletano,' which** translates as **'Neapolitan Nativity/crib scenes.'** The first Nativity scene in Naples is said to have been installed in **the Church of S. Maria del presepe (Saint Mary of the Nativity)** in 1025, long before St. Francis of Assisi popularized Nativity scenes in the world.

In the 16th century, it became common to have Nativity scenes displayed in one's own home, continuing to be popular today. On December 8, Nativity scenes are customarily placed on the mantel. However, it is not until the evening/night of December 24 that the figure of the baby Jesus is placed in the crib/manger.

The Nativity scene is sometimes presented in a pyramid style, which can reach heights of several meters! It's made up of multiple tiers of shelves that have been decorated with colored paper, gold-covered pinecones, and miniature candles, to name a few details. A tiny star is frequently hung inside the top of the pyramid/triangle to represent the sun. Fruit, candy, and presents may also be found on the shelves above the manager scene.

Neapolitan Nativity scenes are unique because they always include extra 'everyday' people and items such as houses, waterfalls, food, animals, and even figures of prominent people. Naples is also home to the world's most extensive Nativity scene, which has over 600 pieces and is the largest in the world!

St. Gregory Armeno Street:

«Via San Gregorio Armeno» (St. Gregory Armeno Street) is a street in Naples where nativity scene manufacturers may still be seen. Beautiful, handcrafted Nativity scene ornaments and figures - as well as whole Nativity scenes - can be purchased on the street.

Food:

On Christmas Eve, it is customary to refrain from eating meat and, in some cases, dairy products too. People frequently enjoy a light seafood supper before going to the Midnight Mass at the church. The varieties of fish served and the way they have presented change from region to region in Italy.

However, Italians prefer sausages and believe that sausages represent wealth and abundance and are cut in a shape that resembles coins.

Getting rid of bad luck:

To ward off bad luck, Italians throw old pots, clothes, and unwanted items from upstairs of their houses, out of their windows. It is a practice of letting go of all the things of the past that are negatively impacting them in some way.

'Panettone':

People often enjoy a slice of Italian Christmas Cake called 'Panettone after returning from the Midnight Mass services, similar to a dry, fruity sponge cake and a cup of hot chocolate when it is chilly weather.

The Feast of the Seven Fishes:

A large Christmas Eve dinner consisting of various fish dishes has become a prevalent tradition for many Italian-American households. **The Feast of the Seven Fishes**, also known as **'Esta dei Sette Pesci'** in Italian, is celebrated every year on the first Sunday of August. The feast appeared to have originated in southern Italy and was brought to the United States by Italian immigrants during the nineteenth century. It appears to be more prevalent in the United States than it is in Italy.

Epiphany and Fairy Befana:

In Italy, the Feast of the Three Kings is also celebrated. Children think that an old lady named 'Befana' will bring them gifts on the night of the Feast of the Three Kings. Befana would fly on her broom, open the door with her golden key and fill the stockings that the children have placed by the fireplace. As for the children who misbehave, Befana brings sweet coal for them. In some places of northern Italy, the Three Kings may bring you gifts rather than Befana, so be prepared. 'Babbo Natale' (Santa Claus) may send them a few little gifts on Christmas Day, but the primary day for gift-giving is on the Feast of the Three Kings (Epiphany).

CHAPTER 6:
PERU AND ECUADOR

PERU & ECUADOR

PEOPLE ASK SHAMANS TO READ FORTUNE
EGG AND BEER FORTUNE TELLING REMAINS POPULAR.

ATTRACTIVE WOMAN
(INSTEAD OF A Christmas tree)
IS DRESSED UP AND DECORATED
WITH FRUITS AND FLOWERS

Christmas is a particular time of year throughout South America, and in Peru, where Christianity is practiced by much of the population, Christmas is a significant event. As a result of the country's enormous population, Christmas is one of the most critical periods of the year there.

While most festivals are comparable to those in Europe and North America, some customs are unique to the country and represent the nation's history and identity. Even if you are not religious, these traditions make Peru a unique destination to spend the holidays. It is difficult not to become swept up in the splendor of Christmas in Peru, making it an excellent time to immerse yourself in the local culture and traditions. It is a terrific opportunity to see a different side of Peruvian life if you travel during the Christmas holidays.

Peruvians and people in other South American countries such as Venezuela and Bolivia consider **Noche Buena,** or Christmas Eve, a noticeably big event in their country.

Attending church on Christmas Eve is a significant element of the holiday festivities. It is customary for Peruvians to attend the **Misa de Gallo,** also known as **Rooster Mass**, which usually begins at 10 p.m., earlier than several other South American countries.

Following the Christmas Eve service, some families begin their Christmas meal at midnight, while others wait until the children have opened their gifts. In any case, both the feast and the opening of presents take place around this time.

Immediately following supper on Christmas Eve, many people hit the streets to say hello to friends and neighbors and continue the festivities. Fireworks are ubiquitous and can be seen throughout the night, even though they are technically prohibited.

Fortune telling with eggs:

An egg is broken into a smooth foggy drink. Whatever patterns appear on the cup predicts a person's fortune. For good luck, one must drink it immediately.

Yellow underwear:

In Peru and Ecuador, wearing yellow underwear on New Year's Eve is said to bring good luck. You need to receive a new pair of yellow underwear as a gift. There are slight distinctions in this custom in different countries. For example, in Peru, you should wear yellow underwear for money and red underwear for love.

Potatoes for financial boost:

The natives place three potatoes under their chair or sofa — one that has been peeled, one that has been half-peeled, and one that has not been peeled. At midnight, a potato is selected at random, and the state of that person and family finances for the following year is predicted. The peeled potato represents ill financial fate, the half-peeled potato represents a typical year, and the unpeeled potato represents a bountiful harvest in the coming year.

Decorations:

The nativity scene is quite famous in Peru and may be found in almost every home. Nativity scenes are frequently big and elaborate (often taking up a whole wall), and they include statues of the Three Wise Men, Jesus in the manger, and other figures from the story of the Nativity. There are times when the typical tableau is given an Andean touch, with llamas and alpacas taking the place of biblical imagery such as donkeys and camels, among other things.

More miniature scenes, known as retablos, are folk art in which religious events are painted or carved in stone or wood, and they are a sort of folk art. Retablos are three-dimensional scenes that are often housed in a rectangular box with two doors on the front. Throughout the year, especially in the mountainous parts of Peru, you can find them for sale in markets and souvenir shops. The scenes featured within a retablo may reflect historical or religious events or depict simple ordinary life scenes. Still, Christmas retablos are most often depictions of the Nativity.

Food:

Food plays an essential role in Peruvian Christmas celebrations, just as it does in other parts of the world. A typical roast turkey meal or **Lechon**, roasted pig, is served after midnight mass prayers, accompanied by various dishes, such as apple sauce and tamales, enjoyed by many families throughout Peru.

Aside from the geographical variants, there are other regional variances, such as fish dishes on the coast and a typical pachamanca in the highlands and wild chicken cooked over an open fire in the jungle.

Adults greet the evening with champagne while children sip hot chocolate flavored with cinnamon and cloves to start the festivities—Peruvians like panetón (**Panettone**), a fruit cake in the Italian dish panettone, for dessert.

Chocolateradas, which are social gatherings in which people meet to sip hot chocolate, is another popular event during the holiday season in Peru, and they are held every year. Chocolateradas for poor communities is held by churches and other community organizations, with free hot chocolate (and panetón) distributed to families as a charitable holiday gift.

Meanwhile, talking about **Ecuadorians (the people in Ecuador)**, most of them do not adorn their homes with Christmas lights, so don't expect to see a riot of color on the streets. Cities and towns, on the other hand, frequently embellish!

Novena de Aguinaldos:
The nine days leading up to Christmas, known as the **Novena de Aguinaldos,** are historically reserved for religious practices. Each day of the novena corresponds to a month of Mary's pregnancy, with the novena culminating with her arrival in Bethlehem and the birth of Jesus at the end of the month. Throughout the novena, the same recitation is used, with the addition of a particular prayer for each day that is specific to that day. These holy days of prayer have evolved into social occasions in many places, providing chances for families, coworkers, and neighbors to gather and celebrate the holiday season with festive drinks and holiday fare.

Food in Ecuador:
Like many other countries throughout the world, Ecuador celebrates Christmas with a plethora of sweets and festive beverages! **Buuelos** are doughnut-like balls of enriched dough deep-fried and served with dark cane syrup, a Mexican specialty.

They are particularly well-known in Ambato, where a festival held in December offers up some of the greatest buuelos in the country.

Mistelas, which are little hard candies filled with a liquor of the same name, is another popular treat.

The Christmas holidays are also when Ecuadorians indulge in roast turkey, roast pork, and even ham. Adding premium ingredients to year-round favorites elevates them to a higher level of excellence — for example, a **ceviche** made with **langostino** instead of shrimp.

Pase del Niño:

Ecuadorians love to enjoy the **Pase del Niño,** celebrated on December 24, Christmas Eve in most villages, and is one of their favorite holidays. Local folks parade through the city's streets with a statue or depiction of Jesus as a kid. Jesus is frequently accompanied by Mary, Joseph, the Three Kings, as well as villagers dressed in traditional attire, bands of traditional musicians, and folkloric dancers, among other people.

Cuenca has one of Ecuador's most well-known **Pase del Niño** processions, while many other cities also participate in some form of this event each year. It is essential to double-check the timetable for staying because certain municipalities perform processions earlier in the season, such as the Province of Bolivar, which celebrates the Pase del Niño 15 days or so before Christmas Eve you arrive. Several smaller Pase del Niño will be held in different local neighborhoods in several cities, such as Quito.

CHAPTER 7:

Christmas in Japan is a joyous and pleasant time of year for the entire country. There are so few Christians in the country that none of the religious implications associated with Christmas were imported from the West, and the holiday is not recognized as a national celebration. In addition to a few distinctive customs exclusively Japanese, many of the items typically associated with Christmas, such as the well-decorated markets and LED lights.

Throughout the winter season, Christmas markets in the European tradition can be seen throughout Japan, from Hokkaido to Kyushu. Everything from delicate tree ornaments to hot cider can be found here.

Susuharai:

It is a house cleaning ceremony at year's end. The term translates into **«brushing off the soot.»** Priests usually beat the dust from the tatami mats and clean up all the house. This also involves the throwing of old and broken household goods, which is a time-consuming task. The concept is that you are getting rid of last year's dust and filth to get carried over into the new year with you.

It is usual to dress for the occasion in brand new clothes.

Food:

In traditional Japanese cuisine, **Toshikoshi Soba**, or year-end soba, is a delicacy of noodles in a heated broth typically served on New Year's Eve and other festive occasions. It is a simple supper that's frequently eaten at home with friends or family. Since there is no established recipe for toshikoshi soba, everyone can make it their way by adding their slight twist.

Mochi is a sort of sticky, gooey rice cake that is popular in Japan. These small round cakes are even utilized in several New Year's decorations, such as the Kagami mochi (Japanese New Year's cake). Traditionally, one of the essential New Year's activities is to make the mochi yourself on New Year's Day. On the other hand, making mochi takes a lot of time and effort, which is why most people prefer to purchase readymade versions.

Kurisumasu Keiki:

From Hokkaido to Kyushu, the traditional Japanese Christmas cake, known as «kurisumasu keki,» may be found on nearly every street corner. Served with finely cut bright red strawberries on top, this delicacy is light and spongy, thanks to whipped cream fillings and icing.

Since Japan's rebirth from the ruins of World War II, this treasured and delectable Christmas dessert, which is also famous for birthday celebrations, has also been regarded as a symbol of wealth.

Decorations:

The most famous and popular monuments in Japan each have their unique holiday illumination displays breathtakingly gorgeous, such as Tokyo Station in the capital, the Kaiyukan Aquarium in Osaka, and the onsen Nabana no Sato is located near Nagashima in the countryside.

From the beginning until the end of the winter season, traditional Christmas markets may be found throughout Japan, from the north to the south.

Kadomatsu:

For the Japanese New Year's occasion, kadomatsu is a decoration made of three cut pieces of bamboo and pine placed on a stand. Immediately following Christmas, you will notice this decorating at the doorways of houses and buildings around Japan. It is thought to be a temporary place for gods, who come to visit and bless the people who live in the dwellings embellished with it. It will remain in place until January 7 before being torched after January 15 to free the gods.

Joya no Kane:

The act of ringing in the new year is known as Joya no Kane, where «Joya» is one way of saying «New Year's Eve» while «kane» means «bell ringing.» One hundred eight times will be rung at Buddhist temples all around Japan, beginning a few minutes before the clock strikes midnight, to commemorate the passing of the Yamato era. Bells are ringing all over Japan as part of one of the essential Buddhist rites of the year, and no matter where you are in the country, you are sure to hear them. The 108 rings signify the Buddhist concept that humans are troubled by 108 different types of earthly cravings and feelings such as hatred and envy and that each striking of the bell removes one of these bothersome desires from your life.

CHAPTER 8:

In French, Happy/Merry Christmas is **'Joyeux Noël,'** and Santa is called **Pere Noel,** who puts Christmas gifts in children's shoes.

The Christmas markets in France are among the most stunning and biggest in Europe, and they are open from November to December. Most of them take place in Eastern France, with the oldest taking place in the picturesque city of Strasbourg and bringing together approximately 300 stalls of artisan food and traditional toys, among other things. The Christmas markets in Colmar and Mulhouse are also incredibly famous since they are beautiful places to soak up the Christmas atmosphere.

Strasbourg, in the north-eastern region of France, hosts one of the most impressive Christmas European markets. The **«Christkindelsmarik»** is what it is known as in the Alsatian language.

Yule Logs:

Yule Logs made from Cherry Wood are often burned in French homes. An old tradition is that the log was carried into the home on Christmas Eve and sprinkled with red wine to make the log smell friendly when it was burning. There is a custom that the log and candles are left burning all night with some food and drinks left out if Mary and the baby Jesus come past during the night.

Food:

The main Christmas meal, called 'Réveillon,' is eaten on Christmas Eve/early Christmas morning after people have returned from the midnight Church Service. Dishes might include roast turkey with chestnuts or roast goose, oysters, foie gras, lobster, venison, and cheeses. For dessert, a chocolate sponge cake log called a bûche de Noël is usually eaten.

Christmas Eve/early Christmas morning is the traditional time for the big Christmas feast known as **'Reveillon,'** to be eaten once individuals have returned from the overnight Catholic Mass.

On January 6, friends, family, schools, and offices throughout the country gather to eat a piece of king cake, known as **«La Galette des Rois,»** with one another.

The Festive Cake:

Also, the king of new years eve is a child who receives a festive cake with some basked bean inside. A King cake is a puff pastry casing filled with frangipane that is sold with a paper crown on top in its most basic form. A tiny little gem is known as a fèvre; French for the bean is concealed within the filling. It is referred known as a bean since it was traditionally used to fill a king cake. These days, you're more likely to come across a figurine made of plastic or porcelain. This year, the individual who discovers the concealed fèvre in their piece of cake will be crowned «king» for the day and will wear a paper crown.

Roast turkey with nuts or roasted goose, oysters, foie gras, lobster, venison, and cheeses are some of the dishes that might be served. A **bûche de Noël,** a chocolate sponge cake log, is traditionally served as a dessert during the holidays.

Another celebration, in some parts of France, is that 13 different desserts are eaten! All the desserts are made from different types of Fruit, Nuts, and Pastries.

Even though every culture celebrates Christmas, the French all go out that when it comes to the holiday season, with seasonal foods lining the shelves and booths of supermarkets and marketplaces. When it comes to preparing the French Réveillon, you'll find various ingredients such as foie gras, oysters, snails, frogs' legs, truffles, and scallops, but you'll also find uncommon meats such as deer, boar, pheasant, and even ostrich. The aim is to eat in a way that is different from the rest of the year because of spending more money on high-end ingredients.

During the large Christmas Eve dinner, all family members get together in large cheerful gatherings at the table to enjoy a lavish meal.

The Christmas Eve:

It is not uncommon for people to go shopping on Christmas Eve in France, unlike in the United Kingdom, where the day is dominated by a last-minute scramble to the shops after work. On the first of the month, the French assemble for a large feast known as Le Réveillon, which comes from the term 'réveil,' which means 'waking.' With a break at midnight, when the youngsters are finally able to open their gifts, the dinner continues late into the night.

Skiing:

If you're spending Christmas in the mountains with your family, there's no better way to cap off the day's festivities than with a solid ski session. The French ski resorts may even be home to some unusual creatures: many individuals enjoy dressing up for their Christmas ski session and whizzing down the slopes, enjoying themselves to the fullest.

If you manage to arrive in France before Christmas Day, there are numerous festivals and activities to enjoy during the winter season. Perhaps the most impressive is Lyon's spectacular Festival of the Lights, where all of the city's structures are brought back to life with music and light performances throughout the night.

CHAPTER 9:

Christmas Eve is an important day in Hungary, and it is known as 'Szent-Este,' which translates as 'Holy Evening.' Families spend the whole time with their families, and they prepare the Christmas Tree in anticipation of the holiday. When only the grownups decorate the tree (and the children are not there), it is a pleasant surprise when the kids come in and discover the tree, and they are informed that angels have delivered the tree specifically for them.

In Hungary, gingerbread is also a traditional Christmas treat that is consumed. Gingerbread is frequently wrapped with brightly colored paper and adorned with Christmas characters throughout the holiday season.

In Hungary, the service of Midnight Mass is top-rated. After their Christmas feast, the vast majority of people attend church.

Food:

Hungarian Christmas dinners are traditionally comprised of fish soup, chicken, or hog as the main course. Typical side dishes include stuffed cabbage, poppy seed rolls, and other sweet pastries to round off the dinner and provide a sweet ending. The Hungarians' favorite sweet, szaloncukor (fondant dipped in chocolate), is available everywhere you go when it comes to dessert.

Festive gift-giving:

On December 6, children get small gifts from **Mikulás**, which are hidden in footwear which have been placed on the sill. The gifts include candies and small toys. Some children will be given switches or twigs from trees in their shoes as a reminder to behave well, in addition to the other modest gifts.

Occasionally, Mikulas appears in the flesh to groups of children. He may be dressed in the traditional bishop's garb or accompanied by helpers representing good and mischief. Ultimately, Mikulas performs a similar function to the Western Santa Claus in that he takes account of the good and bad deeds of children all over the world.

Luca Day:

December 13 is Luca Day, a commemoration of the winter solstice (the longest night of the year). Even though it occurs only 12 days before Christmas, this holiday serves as the official kick-off for holiday gatherings throughout Hungary. The remaining 12 days will be spent by the locals engaging in folkloric practices intended to fend off evil and protect them.

Christmas Eve:

On Christmas Eve, youngsters expect that they will find a gift underneath the Christmas tree for them. They are told that now the presents have been sent by Jesus, who is sometimes referred to as **«Jézuska,»** a nickname or a sweeter version of the name **«Jézus.»** Children gather outside the place where the Christmas tree is located, and then when they hear bells ringing, they are allowed to enter, where they will find gifts under the Christmas tree.

In Hungarian, Happy/Merry Christmas is **'Boldog karácsonyt.'**

While the core family, which includes the children, parents, and grandparents, generally spends Christmas Day together, spending time with the extended family is an essential aspect of the holiday season. On the 25th and 26th of December, aunts, uncles, and friends gather with all of their children to rejoice and spread the Christmas joy, according to tradition.

New year and superstitions:

To ensure good fortune for the future year, people practice rituals around the New Year's celebration. People produce as much noise as they possibly can in an attempt to frighten away evil spirits. Noisemakers such as kazoos, paper horns, and other similar instruments keep the spirits at bay. People frequently dress in ridiculous hats, masks, and accessories, and they purchase items such as noisemakers, pyrotechnics, and sparklers.

Szilveszter:

New Year's Eve in Hungary is called «Szilveszter.» It is traditionally marked by a massive feast of pork and stuffed cabbage, which is believed to bring good luck. To wish your family and friends good luck throughout the year, it is customary to kiss them on both cheeks at midnight (the traditional Hungarian greeting).

CHAPTER 10:

ENGLAND

THEY STAGE SCENES FROM FAIRY TALES, ARRANGE CARNIVALS AND STREET FAIRS

FOR GIFTS, CHILDREN DO NOT PREPARE a *stocking*, AS IN A NUMBER OF COUNTRIES, BUT a *plate*, WHICH THEY PUT ON THE TABLE

THE RINGING OF A BELL THAT SIGNALS THE COMING OF THE *new year*.

Most families decorate their homes with a Christmas tree for the holiday season. The tradition of decorating the Christmas tree is usually a family affair, with everyone participating. Prince Albert, the husband of Queen Victoria, is credited with popularizing Christmas trees in the United Kingdom. Prince Albert was of German descent, and he believed it would be a good idea to incorporate one of his traditions into Christmas celebrations in England.

Decorations:

Holly, ivy, and mistletoe are some of the other plants sometimes used to decorate homes and other structures.

During the Christmas season, most villages, towns, and cities are decked out in Christmas lights. Frequently, they are activated by a well-known person. The most well-known Christmas lights in the United Kingdom can be found on Oxford Street in London. Every year, they grow and sophistic. Thousands of people gather to see the historic 'switch on' ceremony, which takes place around the beginning of November.

Carol Services:

Christmas plays and Carol Services are particularly popular in England during the Christmas season, as they are in many other nations. The church where people primarily worship regularly does a Carols by Candlelight Service, during which only candles are used to illuminate the sanctuary. A very remarkable service that always makes me feel festive and in the mood for the holidays. Carols by Candlelight and Christingle services are held in several other British churches as well.

Santa Claus:

Children think that Father Christmas, sometimes known as Santa Claus, drops gifts in their stockings or pillowcases every Christmas. On Christmas Eve, these are traditionally hung around the fireplace or near the children's beds. Children occasionally leave mince pies and brandy out for Father Christmas to eat and drink when he visits them during the Christmas season. Since Santa will have to drive his sleigh, it's more common for a non-alcoholic beverage to be the last thing on the table.

Father Christmas/Santa Claus receives letters from children listing their wishes, but the letters are occasionally thrown into the fireplace rather than delivered to him via the postal service. After the letters are carried up the chimney, Father Christmas/ Santa reads what is written in the smoke.

Food:

Christmas Pudding is a popular choice for dessert. Mince pies and a plethora of chocolates are also frequently consumed!

Trifle also is a popular dessert option for Christmas dinner and parties.

The dining table is decked out with Christmas crackers for each guest, as well as flowers and candles from time to time.

The United Kingdom is also well-known for its Christmas Cake, which some people adore, and others despise. A classic Christmas fruit cake, covered in marzipan and frosting, and decorated with Christmas-themed cake decorations such as a spring of holly, is baked and served on Christmas Eve.

The Sheffield Carols:

During the weeks leading up to Christmas, certain pubs in North Derbyshire and South Yorkshire (in the north of England) host an exceptional carol singing event, known as 'The Sheffield Carol.' in some of the area's pubs. In that section of England, pubs are commonly found in rural areas or on the outskirts of towns. The songs are frequently relatively local, and variations on the same melody can be found from bar to pub.

Not all of the melodies are about the Christmas tale, as some would think. The taverns are frequently busy, primarily as the holiday season draws more and closer. The singing may be led or supported by folk music performers, an instrument in the tavern, or unaccompanied at times, depending on the circumstances.

CHAPTER 11:

GERMANY

GERMANY

Weihnachtsmärkte

MAGIC OF CHRISTMAS MARKETS
HAS SPREAD FROM
THE GERMAN-SPEAKING PART
OF EUROPE IN THE MIDDLE AGES.

Lebkuchen

THESE BAKED DELIGHTS CONTAIN
HONEY, A NUMBER OF SPICES

Germany's Christmas celebrations are dominated by Advent, which lasts from November to December. Advent calendars are utilized in a variety of ways in German houses, including the following. There are various alternatives to the typical card-based ones used in many nations, such as a wreath of Fir tree branches with 24 ornamented boxes or bags hanging from it. Every box or bag contains a small gift for the recipient. Another style of the Advent wreath is known as an **'Advent Kranz,'** which is a circle of fir branches with four candles in the center. An analogy might be made with the Advent candles, which are sometimes are using in churches. Each week in Advent, one candle is lit just at the start of each new week.

The Christmas Tree:

Germans place a high value on the decoration of their Christmas trees. They were first employed in Germany in the late Middle Ages, according to historical records. According to tradition, the women of the family will normally decorate the trees in secret whether there are young kids in the family. On Christmas Eve, the Crucifix was customarily brought inside the house by the family. On Christmas Eve in various parts of Germany, the family would read the Bible and perform Christmas carols such as O Tannenbaum, Ihr Kinderlein Kommet, and Stille Nacht, among other things (Silent Night).

Decorations:

To make the house appear more attractive from the outside, wooden frames covered with colored plastic sheets containing electric candles are sometimes placed in the windows.

Germany is well-known for its Christmas Markets, where a wide variety of holiday delicacies and decorations are available for purchase. Glass ornaments are perhaps the most well-known of all German decorations. The glass decorations were originally made by hand blowing glass and were introduced into the United States by Woolworth stores in the 1880s. In the United States, the myth of the glass 'Christmas Pickle' is

well-known, although it is only a legend. The Christmas Pickle is something that the majority of the people in Germany haven't ever heard of.

Christmas Eve is the primary day when Germans exchange presents with their families.

In German, Happy/Merry Christmas is **'Frohe Weihnachten.'**

Food:
The Christmas meal is one of the most eagerly awaited German Christmas traditions! The traditional Christmas feast consists of roast duck, geese, rabbit, or a combination of these.

Another food item exceptional for Christmas in Germany is **Plätzchen**, commonly known as **Christmas cookies** in Germany, which are baked throughout the holiday season.

Christkind:
Per custom, the 'Christkind' (Christ kid or Baby Jesus) will put the wrapped presents and parcels underneath the Christmas tree, and young children are typically not permitted to enter the lounge room before the evening celebrations. Consequently, when the children are finally invited into the living room, they are usually highly eager to see the beautifully decorated Christmas tree that has been lit and the gifts that have been placed beneath it. On Christmas Eve, families traditionally gather to read the Christmas story and sing Christmas songs together, followed by a meal and the consumption of traditional 'Christmas Stollen,' a classic German Christmas cake made with raisins and nuts. In addition to decorating the tree together throughout the day, many families with older kids attend midnight mass at their local church once the Christmas activities are completed.

Christmas Day is called **«Erster Feiertag»** ('first celebration'), and December 26 is known as **«Zweiter Feiertag»** ('second celebration').

Nikolaustag:

Nikolaustag, also known as Saint Nicholas Day, is celebrated by families on December 6. In many cases, a 'real' Saint Nicholas, clothed in the traditional red coat and hat and sporting a white beard (to mask the identity of a family friend's father), as well as his scary assistant 'Knecht Ruprecht,' who is clad in black, visit the houses of families that have small children. Their purpose is to inquire about the children about whether or not they have been excellent during the year. They also offer modest goodies to the lovely kids and discipline the wicked ones. Typically, this is a joyous and festive day that is enjoyed with friends and family, and Christmas carols are played during the festivities.

CHAPTER 12:

AUSTRALIA

AUSTRALIA

IN THE COUNTRY OF kangaroos,
THE NEW YEAR IS CELEBRATED NOT IN WINTER,
BUT IN SUMMER.
ONE OF THE PLANET'S LARGEST FIREWORKS IS
LAUNCHED INTO THE SKY AT Sydney Harbor.

Kanguru

While it is customary in Europe to congregate on Christmas Eve, it is more typical in Australia to do so on Christmas Day (December 25). Some people of the community may want to attend mass on Christmas Night or Christmas Day - if this is something you would like to do, there is almost certainly a church in your area that you may visit.

Food:

For those planning a Christmas party, be sure to check your state's gathering regulations for indoor/outdoor gathering restrictions. If you're visiting a specific event, make sure to check the authorized website or social media accounts for the most up-to-date information.

Australians traditionally spend Christmas Day gathering with their closest relatives and friends for a Holiday lunch or dinner in their homes. The lunch is typically comprised of a variety of hot and cold foods and fresh seafood and vegetables. Although Christmas happens during the summer, many families will still enjoy a roast turkey, hot sides, and a decadent Christmas dessert on the actual day of celebration.

If you're having a get-together with a bunch of pals on Christmas Day, you might want to consider hosting a «pot-luck.» Because of this, everybody can bring a portion of food to offer, and the job of hosting does not have to fall solely on the shoulders of one individual.

Also, Australian summer in December means that orchards are in full bloom and that supermarkets and marketplaces are bursting at the seams with sweet and fresh cherries.

Gifts:

In Australia, it is a customary tradition to give or receive presents from friends and family. Most of the time, this is reserved for family and friends. However, you can consider presenting a little surprise or letter to an employer, manager, or anybody else to whom you'd like to express your gratitude.

The Brisbane event:

A giant Christmas tree can be found in Brisbane's King George Square during the lead-up to Christmas, and visitors are encouraged to take a look. The exterior of City Hall is also illuminated with animated projections depicting amusing Australian Christmas stories.

Carols by Candlelight:

Carols by Candlelight, which takes place on Christmas Eve (December 24) in Melbourne, is a fundraising music event broadcast live across the country. Carols by Candlelight is held at the Sidney Myer Music Bowl, and all revenues from the event benefit Vision Australia's charitable effort.

Melbourne's famed Federation Square is transformed into Christmas Square for the holiday season, complete with a giant Christmas tree, a 6-meter-high sparkling bauble that you can take selfies within, free music performances, food trucks, and other festive decorations.

The Boxing Day:

Boxing day, a day following Christmas is typically another day of festivity with family and close friends. The fact that it is yet again another public holiday for most Australians means it is an excellent opportunity for them to unwind, take in the celebrations, and, if they have indulged a little too much the day before, begin the process of getting back on track after the holidays.

The traditional tradition is for individuals to assemble at their friends' homes on Boxing Day to watch the Boxing Day Test after their family celebrations.

The tradition for the Boxing Day Test is to either plan your entire day around the match or entirely ignore it, depending on your perspective.

That goes for Boxing Day bargains and squeezing in just a little bit of extra shopping before the New Year's Eve celebrations get crowded.

The Fall Festival:

The Falls Festival, which takes place in Tasmania and Victoria, is particularly popular with people. Australians with one other a Happy New Year in a festive manner around the country. On January 1, they head to the beach, where they participate in surfing, dancing, and picnicking.

The Christmas Tree:

Since the conventional Christmas trees cannot grow in Australian climate, little metrosideros, a small tree with red flowers, is decorated.

CHAPTER 13:

UNITED STATES

THE SYMBOL OF THE AMERICAN NEW YEAR IS A *BABY* IN A *DIAPER*.

ACCORDING TO TRADITION, IN *12 MONTHS* THE CHILD GROWS OLD AND TRANSFERS HIS RESPONSIBILITIES TO A *NEW BABY*.

SALES ARE TRADITIONALLY HELD ON DECEMBER 31ST. AMERICANS RETURN CHRISTMAS GIFTS TO STORES THAT THEY DON'T LIKE.

As a result of the country's multi-cultural background, the United States boasts a diverse range of Christmas traditions and celebrations. Countries.

Food:
Turkey or ham with cranberry sauce is the typical holiday dish for families in Western European countries. Many Eastern European families enjoy turkey with trimmings, cabbage dishes, and soups, while other Italian families enjoy lasagna.

When it comes to decorating their Christmas Tree, some people in the United States utilize popcorn threaded on a string. Baking gingerbread houses also is a popular Christmas tradition, both to make and to consume. In the United States, eggnog is considered a «traditional» Christmas drink.

Decorations:
Individuals in the United States enjoy decking out the exteriors of their residences with lights and occasionally with figurines of Santa Claus, Snowmen, and Reindeer. On Christmas Eve, some cookies and a cup of milk are frequently left out for Santa to enjoy as a snack.

Christmas is a time when towns and cities decorate their roads with lights to commemorate the holiday. Perhaps the most well-known Christmas streetlamps in the United States are located in Rockefeller Center in New York City, where there is a massive Christmas Tree in front of a public ice-skating rink over the holidays and New Year's Eve.

Mumming:
In some places, cultural traditions such as Mumming are practiced. Mummer's Day Parade takes place on New Year's Day in Philadelphia and lasts for over six hours! Clubs are known as «New Years Associations» put on spectacular performances in elaborate costumes that take months to create. The competition is divided into four categories: comic books, fancy dresses, string bands, and fancy brigades.

Families in small communities along the Mississippi River's levees (high river banks) light bonfires on Christmas Eve to assist 'Papa Noel' in finding his way to the children's homes in the southern part of the state.

UNITED STATES

AT 23:59, A HUGE BALL IS LET GO FROM THE ONE TIMES SQUARE SKYSCRAPER.

IN A MINUTE, IT FLIES 23 METERS, AND THE LAST 10 SECONDS THE TOWNSPEOPLE COUNT DOWN TOGETHER. NEW YEARS COMES WHEN THE BALL TOUCHES THE GROUND.

The Christmas Day:

The most important day of the year in the USA is December 25, also known as Christmas. Traditionally, it is celebrated with a large family supper in Thanksgiving dinner, which includes roast turkey, mashed potatoes, and salty meat pies, among other things.

In addition, it is the day that Santa Claus will visit! That is why families usually gather for breakfast together the following day to open all the gifts he had left for them the night before.

New Year:

In the United States, New Year's Eve is frequently spent with friends and involves many big dinners and parties. As a result, fireworks displays are held in most locations around the country as soon as a new year is officially declared.

A massive ball is thrown from the One Times Square building at 23:59 local time. It travels 23 meters in a minute, and the last 10 seconds are spent counting down with the rest of the community. When the ball lands on the Earth, the New Year celebrations begin.

CONCLUSION

In addition to being a religious holiday, Christmas is also a global cultural and economic phenomenon celebrated on December 25. On this day, December 25, Christians mark the birth of Jesus of Nazareth, a prophet whose teachings serve as the foundation of their faith. Exchanging gifts, decorating Christmas trees, visiting the church, enjoying meals with family and friends, and, of course, waiting for Santa Claus to arrive are all popular holiday traditions to participate in. Since 1870, December 25, sometimes known as Christmas Day, has been observed as a national holiday in the United States.

This book aims to make the children, along with the parents reading, realize that studying and researching different cultures and traditions related to the festive time of Christmas. After reading this book, kids will understand how festivals in general and Christmas are explicitly celebrated across the globe. The children will also develop a habit of understanding, appreciating, and respecting all the countries and ethnicities around the world.

Children will contemplate that cultural experiences provide opportunities for recreation, enjoyment, learning, and sharing experiences with others. They are also opportunities for leisure, entertainment, and learning.

CITATIONS

A True Northern Christmas. (2020, November 19). VisitFinland.Com. https://www.visitfinland.com/article/a-true-northern-christmas/#7911185e

Christmas & winter breaks in Scotland. (2021, February 2). Visit Scotland. https://www.visitscotland.com/holidays-breaks/christmas-winter/

Christmas in Spain - Spanish Christmas Traditions - don Quijote. (2020, November 13). Don Quijote. https://www.donquijote.org/spanish-culture/holidays/christmas/

How is Christmas celebrated in Vietnam? (2020, December 7). Real Word. https://www.trafalgar.com/real-word/how-christmas-vietnam-celebrated/

Curtin, E., & Curtin, E. (2019, December 5). 8 Christmas Traditions in Italy. City Wonders. https://citywonders.com/blog/Italy/Rome/8-italian-christmas-traditions

C. (2018, July 27). Holiday Traditions Around the World: Part 1 - Peru. Cultural Awareness. https://culturalawareness.com/holiday-traditions-around-the-world-part-1-peru/

Drake, A. (2017, December 4). Celebrating Christmas in Ecuador. Not Your Average American. https://notyouraverageamerican.com/celebrating-christmas-in-ecuador/

Joy, A. (2016, November 21). How To Celebrate Christmas In Japan. Culture Trip. https://theculturetrip.com/asia/japan/articles/how-to-celebrate-christmas-in-japan/

Christmas in France: French Christmas traditions | Expatica. (2021, June 4). Expat Guide to France | Expatica. https://www.expatica.com/fr/lifestyle/holidays/christmas-in-france-871680/

Tempus Public Foundation. (2020, December 23). Christmas in Hungary. http://studyinhungary.hu/blog/christmas-in-hungary

Toast, S. (2021, June 8). Christmas Traditions Around the World. HowStuffWorks. https://people.howstuffworks.com/culture-traditions/holidays-christmas/christmas-traditions-around-the-world

Ray, A. (2017, October 30). 15 Christmas Traditions Only Germans Will Understand. Culture Trip. https://theculturetrip.com/europe/germany/articles/15-christmas-traditions-only-germans-will-understand/

Gliku, O. (2020, December 15). Celebrating Christmas in Australia. Insider Guides. https://insiderguides.com.au/celebrate-christmas-australia/

Zamora, C. (2020, December 14). How is Christmas celebrated in the United States? Howlanders. https://www.howlanders.com/blog/en/usa/christmas-united-states/

Shultz, T. (2017, December 8). Feast of the Immaculate Conception. Diocesan. https://diocesan.com/feast-of-the-immaculate-conception/

THE END

Made in United States
North Haven, CT
27 July 2022

21808252R00043